The Art of
OVEREATING

A BELLYFUL OF LAUGHS ABOUT OUR FOOD-PHOBIC CULTURE

LESLIE LANDIS, MFT

STERLING

New York / London

www.sterlingpublishing.com

STERLING and the distinctive Sterling logo are registered trademarks of Sterling Publishing Co., Inc.

2   4   6   8   10   9   7   5   3   1

Published by Sterling Publishing Co., Inc.
387 Park Avenue South, New York, NY 10016
© 2009 by Leslie Landis
Distributed in Canada by Sterling Publishing
c/o Canadian Manda Group, 165 Dufferin Street
Toronto, Ontario, Canada M6K 3H6
Distributed in the United Kingdom by GMC Distribution Services
Castle Place, 166 High Street, Lewes, East Sussex, England BN7 1XU
Distributed in Australia by Capricorn Link (Australia) Pty. Ltd.
P.O. Box 704, Windsor, NSW 2756, Australia

Sterling ISBN 978-1-4027-6456-1

For information about custom editions, special sales, premium and
corporate purchases, please contact Sterling Special Sales
Department at 800-805-5489 or specialsales@sterlingpublishing.com.

Chapter Title Art Credits: Ch1 - Smithsonian American Art Museum, Washington DC/Art Resource, NY; CH2 Réunion des Musées Nationaux/Art Resource, NY; Ch3 - Snark/Art Resource, NY; Ch4 - Réunion des Musée Nationaux/Art Resource, NY; Ch5 - Victoria & Albert Museum, London, Great Britain/Art Resource, NY; Ch6 - Eric Lessing/Art Resource, NY; Ch7 - Tate Gallery, London, Great Britain/Art Resource, NY; Ch8 - Snark/Art Resource NY; Ch9 - Scala/Art Resource, NY; CH10 - Réunion des Musées Nationaux/Art Resource, NY; CH11 - Eric Lessing/Art Resource, NY; CH12 - Banque d'Images, ADAGP/Art Resource, NY; CH14 - Scala/Art Resource,NY; Ch1! - Alinari/Art Resource, NY; Ch16 - Erich Lessing/Art Resource, NY

Photography Credits: PhotoDisc, KPT, istockphoto and Jupiterimages(PhotoDisc, Comstock, Rubberball, Steve McAlister-BrandX, R. Gardette-Stock Image, Dynamic Graphics, Corbis, Thinkstock, Bill Nicholson-Pixland Creasource, Burke/Triolo-BrandX, Image Source White, Image Source Pink, Image Source Black, Liquid Library)

Photo Illustrations: Brian Peterson, Roam Creative

For Martin, with all my love
– Leslie

ACKNOWLEDGMENTS

Thank you, Michael James Jackson and Marc Firestone, for making my dream of being a published author come true.

Thank you, Sean Dennison, for introducing me to Michael Jensen and to Michael Jensen for introducing me to my incredible creative team, Brian Peterson and Laura Grover.

I have a special appreciation for Brian's artistic sensibility and talent and for Laura's style, sensibility and taste. His artwork and many great lines made every idea funnier. Her editing and creative input made any good idea better.

Loving gratitude to my mom, Sylvia Samet, for always believing in me.

Finally, my special thank you and gratitude to my husband, Martin Landis, for his support, encouragement and singular inspiration for this book. It would not exist without him.

Ingredients

Serving Size: As much as you want

PREFACE

THE "BIG" SCARE

Back in the days before diets became "lifestyle" choices, and healthy food programs became a national obsession, eating was the one activity that we all had to do that was also pleasurable, and even fun. *The Art of Overeating* was written as a response to our food phobic culture. Taking a humorous look at our collective eating foibles can also become part of the solution. After all, you can't stuff your face when you are laughing. The deep and meaningful message of this book is:

"Have your cake and read it too."

The Art of
OVEREATING

CHAPTER 1
THE "BIG" PICTURE

"*Give me liverwurst or give me death!*"

The BIG OL' U.S. of A.

The land of double cheeseburgers, jumbo sodas, and triple decker clubs. A continent measured in yard-long subs, foot-long hot dogs and mile-high pancakes, filled with the economic benefits of 2-for-1 pizza and all-you-can-eat buffets. The whole enchilada. The BIG TAMALE...

For an overeater, the best place to live is the United States. In America, you can generally count on extra large plates overflowing with humongous portions. This makes overeating not only convenient and easier, but also natural.

No wimpy amount of food on tiny dinner plates as you find in Europe and other continents. In the U.S., men, women and children are all given an amount of food suitable for an elephant.

MAXIMIZE THE OVER-MAXIMIZED

There are certain rules to follow:

⭐ NEVER SHARE

This particularly applies to the family style restaurant where you are expected to share. That platter sized bowl of pasta is all yours if you ordered it. Chinese restaurants are an exception to this rule. They provide the perfect opportunity to order lots of extra dishes allowing you to eat extra amounts of each.

⭐ NEVER GIVE IN

When confronted by an aggressive dinner companion seeking to invade your plate, a strategic fork to the knuckle will usually get your point across.

⭐ NEVER DELAY

Don't take home anything in a doggie bag unless you plan to eat it as soon as you leave the restaurant as well-thought-out nourishment for the trip home—or you're currently studying origami and have yet to master the foil swan.

⭐ NEVER BE SLOPPY

Always clean your plate. The dishwasher works for minimum wage. Don't make his job any harder than it already is by leaving bits of food, smears of sauce or unwanted garnish. Lick your plate clean if necessary.

⭐ NEVER DISCARD

As you've always been told, there are always children starving somewhere in the world, so it's a sin to waste your waist.

⭐ NEVER COMPROMISE

If you do find yourself traveling in a country that only provides minuscule portions, make it a "normal" American meal by ordering at least 2 entrees . . . or maybe 3 . . . or 4. When in Rome, do as the Americans do.

Don't let anyone tell you that overeating is selfish. It actually is just the opposite. Consider that it is estimated that Americans dispose of thirty million tons of food waste every year. That amounts to over one pound of discarded food per day per person. How selfish is that? So save the environment. Eat everything you order. Eat other people's leftovers. Let no doggie bag go wasted. Eat everything in your refrigerator.

EAT, EAT, EAT

Remember, it's a cause bigger than you, so be as big as you can be about it.

Overeating Is Normal

If overeating isn't normal, then why are obesity rates rising worldwide? Oh sure, there may be a few places left on earth where overeating is not on the rise. But as soon as American fast food chains reach a critical mass in those countries, that will change. So stand proudly. You are a member of the expanding majority.

Remember, only YOU are in charge of how much YOU eat. Portion CONTROL means that YOU CONTROL how much YOU eat. Make each portion as big as possible. Ensure the future of the human race. EAT AND BE MERRY!

WHEN TO EAT

Anytime is a good time to **EAT**.
When the sun is up, **EAT**.
When it's cloudy, **EAT**.
When you can't sleep, **EAT**.

Don't worry about whether you're hungry or not, just eat anytime you want. In fact, the more you eat and the more often you eat, the less hunger is a factor. Not only will you not be able to tell if you're hungry, you will always be hungry. You will always feel like eating.

9

FOOD FACTS SPREAD

The ancient Greeks were the first to chew gum.

Food facts to know and share—spread the word around.

In the 1800s, European emigrants traveling to America on the German Hamburg Line ships were served grilled meat patties placed between two pieces of bread.

Das ist es! The hamburger!

CHAPTER 2
BIG LOVE

"*Honey makes the world go 'round.*"

FOOD IS LOVE

When you look at food, you see "love." When you pass the deli counter, every liverwurst is screaming out, *"I love you!"* Every salami, *"Te amo!"* Your very first meal was mother's milk. Always available, provided with love, a never-ending faucet of vitamin-enriched goodness. All your childhood foods were made for you by Mom or Dad with lots of love. You were even encouraged to have a second helping of love in the form of more roast beef, extra carrots, another serving of potatoes au gratin and creamed spinach.

The more food you consume, the more you are filling yourself up with love. Always there, always dependable, always nurturing. Food never rejects you, leaves you or lets you down. A double chin and a spreading midsection are really layers and layers of love.

14

You Are So Delicious!

Honey Bun, Cupcake, Sweetie Pie, Cream Puff, Sweet Pea, Muffin, Peanut Pumpkin Pie, Peaches. All pet names we call someone we love. More proof that you can't eat excessively any more than you can love excessively.

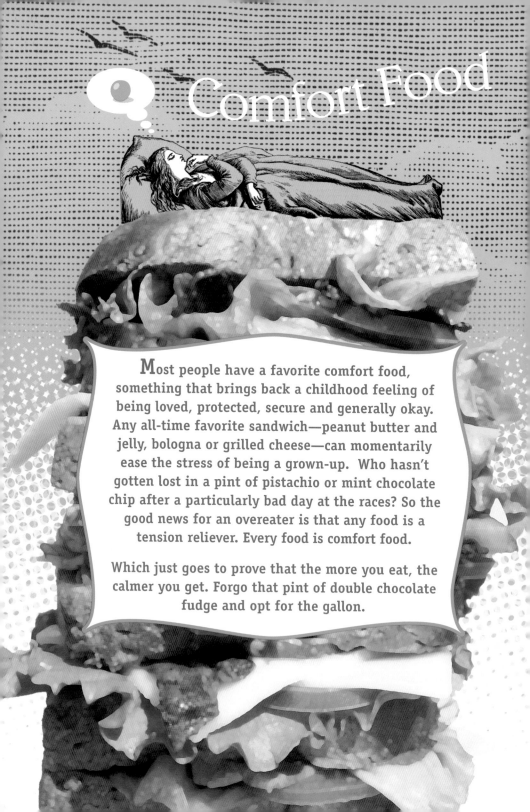

Comfort Food

Most people have a favorite comfort food, something that brings back a childhood feeling of being loved, protected, secure and generally okay. Any all-time favorite sandwich—peanut butter and jelly, bologna or grilled cheese—can momentarily ease the stress of being a grown-up. Who hasn't gotten lost in a pint of pistachio or mint chocolate chip after a particularly bad day at the races? So the good news for an overeater is that any food is a tension reliever. Every food is comfort food.

Which just goes to prove that the more you eat, the calmer you get. Forgo that pint of double chocolate fudge and opt for the gallon.

ANXIETY
▼
Wedding
Cake

FEAR
▼
Mini Rainbow
Marshmallows

PITY
▼
Petit Fours

BLISS
▼
Macadamia
Nuts

GUILT
▼
Lox

SUSPICION
▼
Black
Licorice

INDECISION
▼
Yogurt
Pretzels

SHOCK
▼
Salt & Vinegar
Chips

Emotional Eating

People talk about emotional eating with a negative connotation: *"Oh, she's upset, so she's eating." "He's eating because he's worried."*

What's so "#$@!?%" wrong with that?!

If someone is sad, anxious or unhappy, what could be better than eating? A nice fat slice of chocolate cream pie never made anyone feel worse. A perfectly prepared pot roast can only result in tears of joy. Who knew you would find all that in the refrigerator! Pay no attention to those killjoys who tell you that you must deal with your problems in a more constructive way. What could be more constructive than eating? After all, you're creating a whole new body, maybe even another you ... if you double your size.

DREAD
▼
Beef Jerky

LUST
▼
Honey

ENNUI
▼
Corn
Flakes

HUMILITY
▼
Pie

ELATION
▼
Chocolate
Sprinkles

GREED
▼
Prime Rib

JEALOUSY
▼
Minty
Toothpicks

DOUBT
▼
Mochaccino
Decaf

APATHY
▼
Unsalted
Saltines

YOU'VE EARNED IT!

NICELY DONE!

THAT WAS TOUGH!

ATTA-BOY!

REWARD YOURSELF!

Eating is probably one of the most accessible and least expensive ways you can reward yourself. Any kind of food will work as long as it's something you really like. Of course, if you're an overeater, there are lots of foods you really like.

There's no doubt that for many, dessert is the best reward of all. When you are rewarding yourself, you can eat as much as you want. As much chocolate cake, as much ice cream, as much cheese cake, as much pie—as much as you like.

What should you consider worth a reward? Consider all the difficult things you accomplish every day. You get out of bed. Reward time. Feed your pet. Reward time. Take care of your family. Reward time. Show up at work. Reward time. Drive home in traffic. Reward time. Let's face it, just living deserves a reward.

REWARD OTHERS

It pays to be a generous friend. When at a stadium event, always offer to get the drinks and food from the concession stand. While you are there, you can inhale an extra two or three jumbo dogs. When you get back with everyone's orders, you can pass out extra unrequested goodies such as candy, pretzels and cookies. Of course, you're entitled to more than your fair share, considering you bought and brought it all. If you manage to get treats that no one wants, then all the more for you. This also works at movies, concerts and so many other situations.

CHAPTER 3
BIG ISSUES

"*Two breads are
better than one.*"

ADDICTED TO FOOD?

How can a person be addicted to food? You have to eat to live. You also have to breathe to live, and do you ever hear people being accused of being addicted to breathing?

Let's be fair. If eating can be an addiction, why are there food shows all over TV, cooking demonstrations in stores and cooking classes everywhere? Why is it legal for billboards, magazine ads and TV commercials to hawk food, food, food? No one goes to jail for eating too much food.

SPICY DOGS

BBQ CHIPS

ROOT BEER

the noble act of overeating

Overeating is a noble and unselfish act. As you put away gargantuan amounts of food, those sharing the meal with you will be so put off by your example that they will order less, eat less and pass on dessert. You are improving their well being, so the reality is that your overeating is a wonderful, caring sacrifice.

The extra added bonus—for you—is that when the check is evenly split between all parties, each person will pick up a greater share of your meal. This is truly an example of having your cake and eating it too.

23

Or, Ennui To Go, Please!

Eating when you are bored is a legitimate activity that makes perfect sense. It can be time-consuming and totally involving. You must get yourself to a restaurant, food outlet or grocery store. Once there, study the menu or peruse the aisles. All this takes time and energy, which means calories are burned and you're entitled to a bigger food reward. That's especially true if you have to bring your food home and prepare it. Don't belittle the effort expended to plop it on a plate and pop it into the microwave.

FOOD FACTS

Eight insect legs are found
in the average chocolate bar.

TOP 10
REASONS WHY
PEOPLE SHOULD OVEREAT

1. Instant gratification saves time.

2. Aren't we supposed to end world hunger?

3. Why cut pork when the government won't?

4. Grow the economy and yourself.

5. The U.S.A. can still be No. 1 in something!

6. Excess is a normal American trait.

7. It is good exercise for your jaw.

8. You won't have to fight temptation.

9. Overeaters get a lot of attention.

10. It sure does taste good.

CHAPTER 4
BIG GAINS AND BIG TECHNIQUES

" There is a time and plate for everything. "

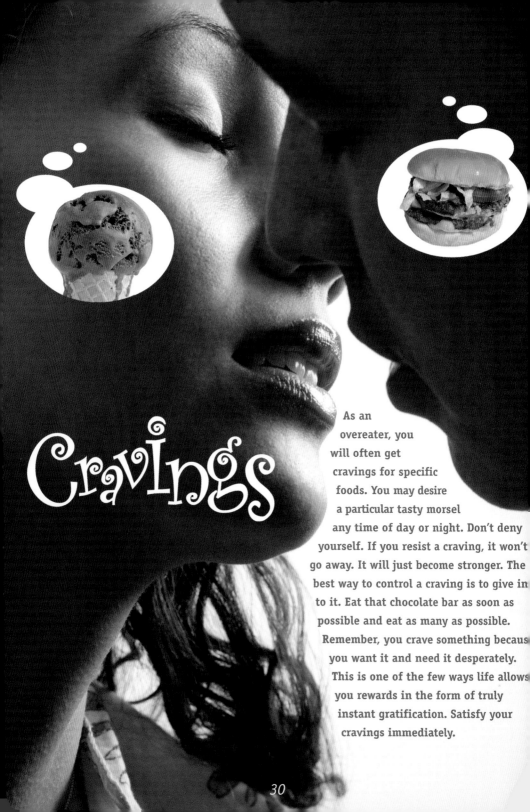

Cravings

As an overeater, you will often get cravings for specific foods. You may desire a particular tasty morsel any time of day or night. Don't deny yourself. If you resist a craving, it won't go away. It will just become stronger. The best way to control a craving is to give in to it. Eat that chocolate bar as soon as possible and eat as many as possible. Remember, you crave something because you want it and need it desperately. This is one of the few ways life allows you rewards in the form of truly instant gratification. Satisfy your cravings immediately.

THE WEIGH-IN CHALLENGE

Never weigh yourself. It might discourage you from eating.

If Challenged, Fight Back!

If you must weigh yourself, use a scale that can be set back at least twenty pounds. Or find one with very small, difficult to read numbers. Then you can imagine any weight you want. If you wear glasses, never wear them when you have to weigh yourself. That way, with a little squinting, your weight is perfect. On a wave of euphoria, you can eat an extra amount that day.

Brutus

Schatzi

Trapper

Rusty

Grazing I

If you've ever had the occasion to walk a dog, you know that dogs engage in a practice commonly known as "grazing." Anything dogs find during the walk that is passably edible, they eat it so quickly that it is usually impossible to stop them. That's how smart dogs are. You can be just as smart.

Max

Britney

Rob

Dave

Phil

Jennifer

D I P

GRAZING II

Another aspect of grazing is near continual eating. Trips to the kitchen for refills need only be interrupted by the need to use the bathroom. Otherwise, eating breaks are built into every aspect of life. That's why there are commercials on the TV, concession stands at the movies, long commutes, coffee breaks near high calorie vending machines and hunger pangs after sex. Happy grazing on the trail of life.

Donuts	2 mi.
Chili Fries	1 mi.
Ice Cream	$\frac{1}{2}$ mi.

NOOKS &CRAN NIES

Drawers, shelves, cabinets and cupboards exist for a purpose. They are perfect places to stash food. If you open a drawer, you will find underwear and *candy bars*. If you open a file cabinet, you will find files and *donuts*. If you reach for a sweater on a shelf, you will find mohair and *potato chips*. Food should be conscientiously squirreled away in case you are too far from the kitchen. Also, if a concerned loved one is monitoring the fridge, you can avoid starvation with your well-placed goodies. Just don't forget to save an ample drawer for the wrappers, bags, crumbs and boxes.

TV
TIDBITS

Overeating and TV viewing are perfectly compatible. If you are consuming while watching, whether it's a snack or a meal, be sure to have lots of food within reach of the remote. That way, you won't have to interrupt your viewing—or your eating.

Beddy-Bye Time

You can do anything in bed—read, watch TV, make love, sleep and EAT. In fact, it's the perfect place to eat. The ancient Romans always ate while reclining. It must aid digestion since food doesn't have to rush from one end to the other. Of course, if you share your bed, you're likely to get an objection. Just remind your bedmate that you only eat on your side. Any crumbs, chunks of chicken or shreds of lettuce that fall between the sheets will be handy when you get hungry during the night.

CHAPTER 5

THE BIG ELEPHANTS
IN THE ROOM

*"A friend who will feed
is a friend indeed."*

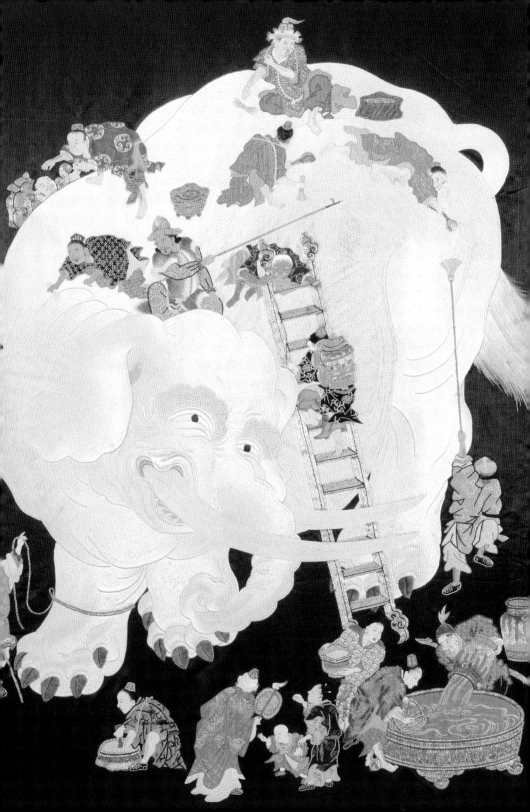

THE FOOD POLICE

CP-58362

DEPT. OF FINGER FOODS – CHEESE OR CHEESE FLAVORED DIVISION

CASE#

SUSPECT Peterson, Brian

BRAND generic cheese-flavored puffs

LOCATION alley behind liquor store on 7th

EVIDENCE: Suspect found behind dumpster with three empty bags and a fourth in his hand. "My gums are numb," he said. Noticed excessive molar build-up.

LEFT HAN

1.Thumb

2.Index Finger

3.Middle Finger

4.Ring Finger

5.Small F

RIGHT

6.Thumb

7.Index Finger — suspect had licked clean before apprehension

8.Middle Finger — licked clean

9.Ring Finger

10.Sm

The food police are all those who try to take the fun out of eating. They are the nutritionists, the dietitians and the government departments that issue food pyramids, regulate product labels and ban soda machines from schools. They claim it is for our well being, our health. But obviously, this is an evil conspiracy to take away our freedom to eat anything we want in any amount we want. Overeaters unite!

"Yes, Dear."

The Importance of a "Co-Dep"

Your very own personal food police is the all-important "co-dep." By definition, a co-dependent person makes (obsessive) efforts to control the errant behavior of someone else. This is not necessarily a bad thing. In other words, a co-dep is anyone who cares enough about you to nag you to no end, especially about food.

Many overeaters already have one or more co-deps in their lives. If you don't have one, get one! A co-dep helps you to keep focused on your zeal for overeating. They provide a challenge, which makes overeating even more rewarding. You have a foil to outsmart and, of course, you're doing your co-dep a favor. They need you to maintain your gluttonous behavior or there will be no point in being a co-dep . . . maybe even no purpose to his or her life. Think of overeating as the key to maintaining your relationship.

I'm with→ Co-Dep

With this in mind, it is important to ask, on a regular basis, for help in policing your eating. There is nothing a co-dep likes better than someone who can't help

Managing
Your Co-Dep

A co-dep gives you articles on dieting, healthy eating and all the illnesses you will get from your poor nutrition. Always thank your co-dep. Reassure him or her that you will read it as soon as you have time. Don't throw the articles out. File them. You can always point to the folder when your co-dep accuses you of not taking them seriously.

45

THINGS I SHOULD EAT

THINGS I SHOULDN'T EAT

BEFORE + AFTER PHOTOS

REASONS I HATE MY CO-DEP

NEW DESSERTS TO TRY!

A co-dep routinely monitors your meals and eating habits. When they are critical, remember that the best defense is a good offense. Always argue. The best arguments are ones such as, "The portions aren't really that big." "It's not as much as it seems." "Everyone else is eating the same amount." Or that you're starved ... you haven't eaten since dinner the night before ... since breakfast ... since your last snack. You get the idea.

Usually a co-dep will be constrained if there are others at the table. After all, constant harping on your food intake makes them appear to be co-dependent. Use this to your advantage. Suggest that everyone pass around their plate for a tasting. Take extra large helpings when it comes to you.

Co-Deps &
Dessert

Dessert is a special category. A co-dep will object to you having any dessert except sorbet. Always insist that you will just have a little taste. Then distract your co-dep with conversation while you quickly eat it all. Eating fast is always a good strategy.

"That's fascinating, and then what happened?"

"Tell me more about your mother."

"Look! Isn't that that chick from that film with that guy from that show that you used to watch with what's-her-name?"

"I have a surprise. Close your eyes and count to a hundred."

"You're getting *verrrry* sleepy."

"I think you dropped your napkin."

"You might want to go fix your makeup."

"Honey, I'm a bit chilly, will you be a doll and get my sweater out of the car?"

"Can you believe she's wearing those shoes with that belt?"

"I'd feel better if you'd call the babysitter one more time."

CHAPTER 6
BIG OCCASIONS

"*To everything there is a seasoning.*"

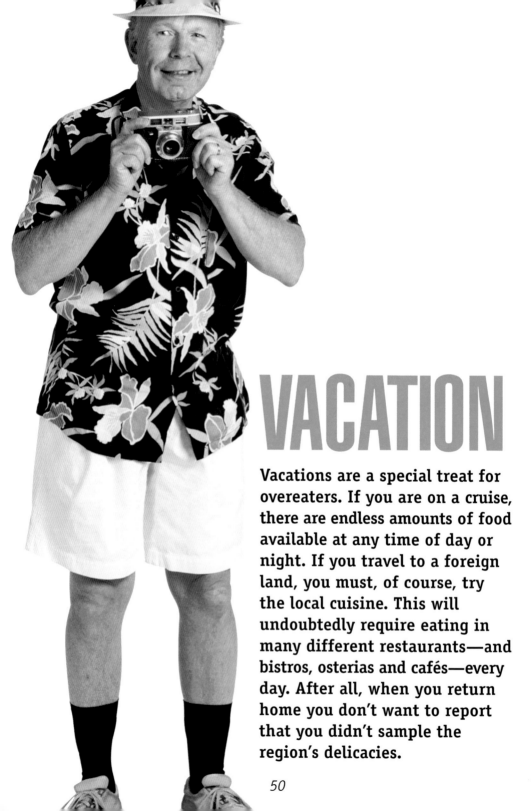

VACATION

Vacations are a special treat for overeaters. If you are on a cruise, there are endless amounts of food available at any time of day or night. If you travel to a foreign land, you must, of course, try the local cuisine. This will undoubtedly require eating in many different restaurants—and bistros, osterias and cafés—every day. After all, when you return home you don't want to report that you didn't sample the region's delicacies.

FOOD FACTS

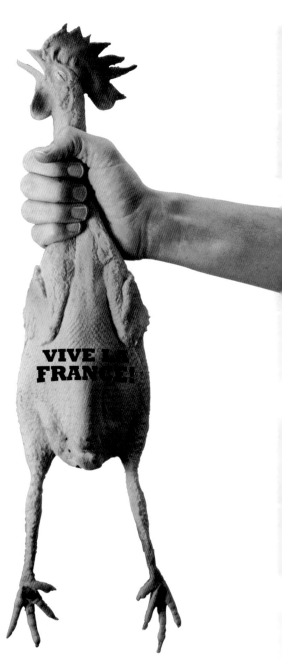

Chicken Marengo was the dish served to Napoleon Bonaparte after every battle

VIVE LA FRANCE!

Sadie Hawkins Day!

Flag Day!

Arbor Day!

Lantern Festival!

You don't need a holiday such as Thanksgiving or Christmas for an excuse to overeat. You can overeat anytime.

On the other hand, a holiday is a great excuse for overeating. After all, when else is it acceptable, even encouraged, to try two, three, four different desserts, even sample a bit of every frosted, baked and rum-buttered recipe on the buffet table? And that's without worrying about the ten tons of calories. It's a special day. Treat yourself.

If you look carefully at a really thorough calendar, you will realize that there is a holiday for something almost every day of the year, especially if you are ecumenical. So don't miss the holidays of every religion and every country. Why not celebrate Election Day with chocolate layer cake? Why not honor Administrative Professionals Day with a 12-pound lobster dripping in butter? Every day can be a feast if you are open-minded.

Tomb Sweeping Day!

Bastille Day!

Day After Tomb Sweeping Day!

Cupcake Day!

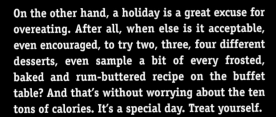

Other Affairs
FOR WHICH YOU'LL BE
Remembered

Weddings, formal parties, Bar Mitzvahs. Whatever the occasion, ingenuity is required. Assess the food flow traffic pattern immediately. Always stand by the kitchen door so you can grab the whole tray of hors d'oeuvres before the server gets to the other guests. Insist that you are taking care of a special group of elderly or infirm people.

A Perfect Dinner Guest

Anyone brave or foolish enough to invite you for dinner already knows that you will want extra heaping helpings of everything. If they haven't planned ahead, then it's their fault if there isn't enough food for everyone else.

It is important to always show impeccable manners. Should a last tasty morsel be left on a platter, first inquire if anyone else would like to eat it. Before there is time for a response, deftly spear it with your fork. Everyone will be too astounded by your speedy precision to even think of objecting.

SCORING BROWNIE POINTS

To really rank in the great guest hall of fame, always volunteer to clean up after a meal at someone's house. After all, since the host provided all the food—it's the least you can do. And think of all the delicious leftovers. Insist on clearing the dishes and washing them by yourself. That way you can lick everyone's plate clean.

If anyone sees you, tell them you believe in saving water.

CHAPTER 7

BIG ADVENTURE

"Diners are a girl's best friend."

HOLY MENU

THE JOY & ART OF EATING OUT

The wonderful thing about dining out is all the courses that a restaurant offers—the bread, the appetizer, the soup, the salad, the fish entrée, the pasta entrée, the meat entrée, the dessert. Be sure to order from every category—the primi and the secondi and beyond—and don't be timid about having more than one dish from each. If anyone objects, insist that you are tasting these selections for future reference. Then sample a huge forkful of each one, many times.

King Crab Version

HOW TO ORDER AT A RESTAURANT

Restaurants today are one of your greatest allies. Most will accommodate your special requests. If you desire pasta prepared with butter instead of olive oil or tomato sauce, just ask for it. The same is true for fish and meat. Why settle for a low-fat, tasteless sauce when you can have a rich, flavorful topping of cream sauce or gourmet gravy. And when you order it that way, have them pour it on. Ask for extra. Smother your food. That is the whole point of sauce. Likewise, when the parmesan cheese is brought to the table, have it shoveled onto your plate.

Salad dressings are a special realm for overeaters. Many restaurants will provide delectable, extra rich ingredients such as cheeses, bacon, mayonnaise and cream.

And never pass up the extras that cost a few "cents" more. Why eat plain pasta when you can add the chicken and the sausage and the shrimp and the . . .

Take Out Take-Out

With take-out, you're not limited to eating in just one place. You can go from restaurant to restaurant to restaurant. Your only limitation is getting it all home. If you have a car, you can order as much food as you can stuff into it. If you don't have a car, you can get a wheelbarrow or a big red wagon and fill it up. The exertion involved in this smorgasbord endeavor means you are entitled to eat everything as soon as you get home.

Finally, don't forget to save the best for last.

Many cultures believe chocolate is an aphrodisiac . . .
helping us to multiply like bunnies.

CHAPTER 8
THE BIG TRIP

*"All roads lead
to ravioli."*

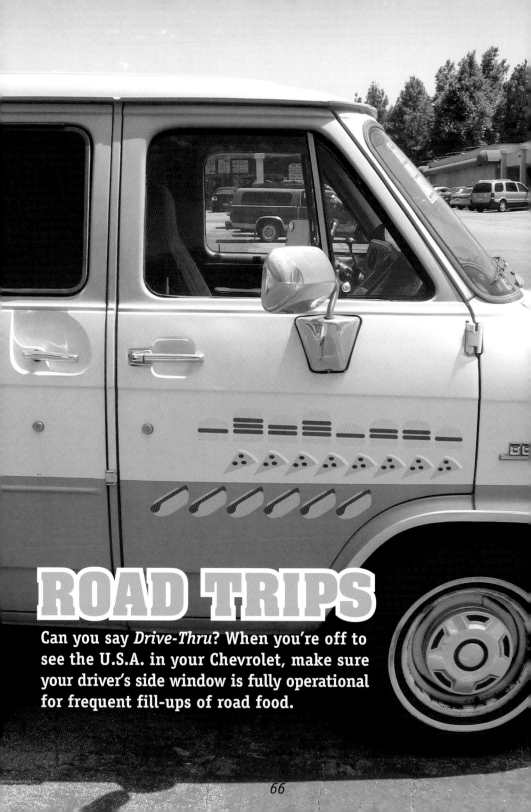

ROAD TRIPS

Can you say *Drive-Thru*? When you're off to
see the U.S.A. in your Chevrolet, make sure
your driver's side window is fully operational
for frequent fill-ups of road food.

DRIVING TO NIRVANA

If they say that getting there is half the fun, why don't cars have refrigerators, microwaves and toaster ovens? If they can cram those electronics into the dashboard, why can't they figure this one out? Yes, navigation systems are great for finding the nearest pizza place, but think of how hungry you'll get on the way there. Surely, there would be no road rage if everyone was happily chowing down en route. After all, a traffic jam would provide a nice opportunity to prepare an extra-special snack. And changing a flat tire would be a perfect occasion for a roadside picnic.

FLYING FOOD

The bad news is that a lot of airlines no longer serve food in coach. The good news is that they still haven't banned you from bringing your own. You're allowed two carry-ons—a small suitcase and a briefcase, laptop case or handbag. Choose wisely about what you'll need in-flight. If you bring enough food, you can eat from the minute you board till the second you deplane. Ditch the clothes and work supplies and stuff your bags with food. The longer the flight, the more you'll need, so pack accordingly. Cram every compartment with treats. Maybe you can even get a smile from the flight attendant if you share your cookies or your cake or your pie or your pot roast or your chicken or your spare ribs or . . .

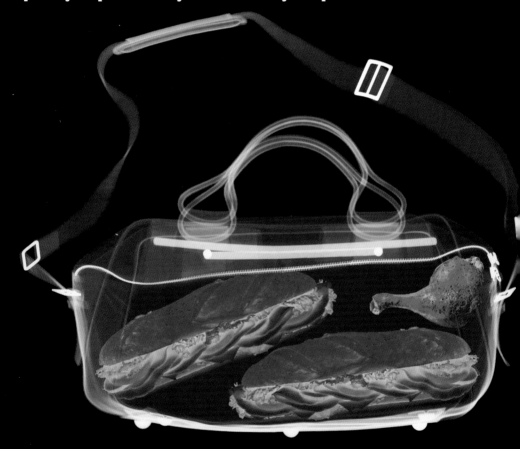

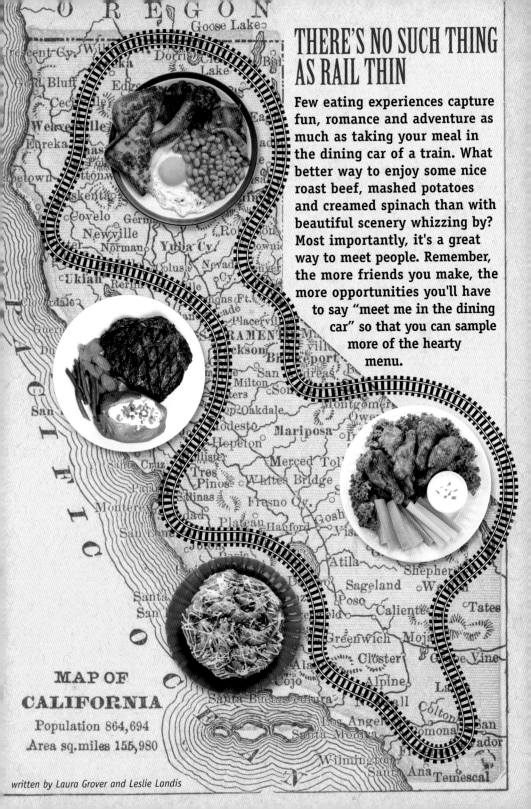

THERE'S NO SUCH THING AS RAIL THIN

Few eating experiences capture fun, romance and adventure as much as taking your meal in the dining car of a train. What better way to enjoy some nice roast beef, mashed potatoes and creamed spinach than with beautiful scenery whizzing by? Most importantly, it's a great way to meet people. Remember, the more friends you make, the more opportunities you'll have to say "meet me in the dining car" so that you can sample more of the hearty menu.

MAP OF
CALIFORNIA
Population 864,694
Area sq. miles 155,980

written by Laura Grover and Leslie Landis

Cruising Along

A cruise ship is a great way to travel. Cruising doesn't mean seeing exotic sights at every port, dancing, sunbathing, gambling and drinking. It means the shipboard romance of cruising to every meal and every snack and lingering as long as possible at the buffet table. Cruising is where you can gain ten pounds and everyone thinks it's normal. So enjoy the fulfilling experience of cruising.

FOOD FACTS

One airline saved $40,000 in 1987 by eliminating one olive from each salad in first class.

CHAPTER 9

BIG IS BEAUTIFUL

"I am the master of my plate and captain of my bowl."

· SVÆ · XLIX

THE CULINARY ARTS

Don't be afraid to cook. Cooking is defined as the preparation of food for eating. Under this definition, opening a bag of potato chips can be considered cooking.

Tasty Hot Pork Sandwiches ...in Minutes!

Mrs. Grover

SERVING SUGGESTION

BROWN GRAVY WITH SLICED PORK

If, however, you apply yourself to the pots and pans routine, you have the great benefit of using any ingredients in any amount. That means you can add as much butter, cream, nuts, cheese, sugar, chocolate, bacon or anything else that you want. You're the chef. Bon appétit!

SUPERMARKET SHOPPING

Forget the fruits and veggies. Go straight to the juicy red meat department, the aisle of salty snacks, the freezer of cheesy pizzas, the floor to ceiling display of cookies. The choices for an overeater are endless.

The deli counter delights with mac 'n' cheese, creamy potato salad, creamier rice pudding, fabulous fried chicken, barbecued beef ribs, Swedish meatballs and french onion soup. The bakery is a cornucopia of chocolate cake, cheesecakes, fruit pies, eclairs and napoleons. For an overeater, the whole store is heaven, with the rare exception of the produce department. Avoid it.

FOOD FACTS

The ripeness of cranberries
is determined by bouncing them.
A well-ripened cranberry can be
dribbled like a basketball.

FOOD FACTS

You will eat the weight of
about six full grown elephants
during your lifetime.

Nutritional Fun Facts

Serving Size: 1 sitting
Servings Per Container: You Decide

	% Daily Happiness
Calories: 3000 Calories from Fat: OK	
Total Fat: 75g	
Saturated Fat: 54g	100%
Trans Fat: 21g	100%
Cholesterol: 250mg	100%
Sodium: 1250mg	100%
Total Carbohydrate: 66g	100%
Dietary Fiber: 0g	100%
Sugars: 123g	100%
Protein: 32g	100%
	100%

100% Daily Happiness
(Buy a box for tomorrow!)

THE BEST "READ"

Always read the labels on foods. They will tell you exactly what you need to know in order to make an informed purchase. Obviously, the foods with the highest fat content, particularly saturated fat, will taste the yummiest. The same applies to products with a high sugar or high salt content. Not only will the labels help you decide what to buy, but reading them will make you hungry!

Don't be put off by foods that claim to be "healthy" or "low fat." Just think outside the box—or can or bag. Remember that a true serving portion is the whole container. If you multiply the fat, sugar and salt content of what is claimed to be a single serving by everything inside, it is likely that the food will be rich and tasty. For maximum effect, eat the entire package all at once.

FAT BOY

NEW! HOMESTYLE LIME-SWISS

LUV NUTZ!

SALTY DEEP-FRIED CREME-FILLED CANDY-COATED FOOD PRODUCT

Just Like Mom Used To Manufacture!

CHAPTER 10
THINK (VERY) BIG

"One good turnover deserves another."

Food Dreams

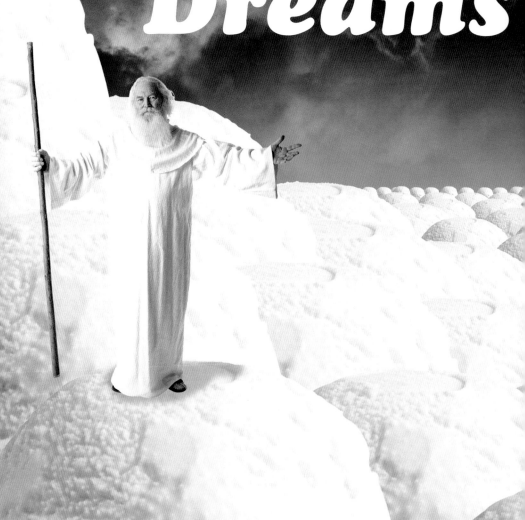

If you are having dreams about food, don't feel guilty. Food dreams are a normal part of being an overeater. A good thing about food dreams is that no one knows what you are imagining, so by all means, get carried away. Your co-dep can't even detect what's going on in your subconscious brain—unless you smack your lips all night. Just check the kitchen first thing in the morning for telltale signs that maybe you were having more than a dream ...

EATING HEALTHY

The best way to eat healthy is to eat everything in large quantities. How else can you be sure that you are getting all the vitamins and minerals you need?

One cake = 7% RDA of Zinc

14.28 cakes = 100% RDA of Zinc. Get busy.

CALORIES **VS** FAT

Why take a chance?
Your body needs
calories and it needs
fat. Eat as much as
you can of both.

BIG VOCABULARY

The most beautiful words in any language:
ice cream, sugar, cake, barbecue, dessert, butter, chocolate, potato chips, cookies, stuffing and candy

Whisper, *no*, **shout!** these sweetest of somethings into the ears of everyone you care about.

And, don't forget the most beautiful
sounding word of all:

Buffet

Often paired with the
wonderfully expressive phrase

"All you can eat"

it is a French term that means you can go back
for as much food as many times as you want.

What could be better than that?

C'est Magnifique!

(Please take a clean plate.)

CHAPTER 11

BIG RATIONALIZATION

“*Birds of a feather
flambé together.*”

If the Genes Fit...

It's true that genetics play a major role in how much you eat and how large you become. That can also be another important reason to eat a lot. You want to be true to your family and body type. If your kin are big people and big eaters, then that is your destiny and it is your duty to fulfill it. You were meant to be a big person.

You were probably given a head start as a child with heaping plates, rich sugary snacks and encouragement to eat additional helpings of everything. Genetics and behavior are your birthright, your legacy. Celebrate your family tradition!

And if you came from a family of thin folks who barely ate enough to stay alive, don't fret. This is your chance to break the mold and correct that. Besides, certainly someone in your family tree long, long ago had a metabolic imbalance and now you have inherited it. It's fate.

1=1

At the very least, a portion of food should be one of anything. It is just fine to eat one watermelon, one Bundt cake, one pie, one bag of chips, one chicken, even one cow. You get the idea.

(CANDY)
APPLE

A Lifestyle Change

Nutritionists say that most people need to eat a lot more fruits and vegetables. If you are not ingesting your fair share, you should make this important modification. Eat as many pectin-packed fruit pies as you can. Eat as many cherry-topped tarts and pineapple upside-down cakes as you can. Vegetables and fruits are so good for you and they are just delicious—especially when added to puddings, potatoes, roasts and risotto.

CARROT
(CAKE)

exercise, take the bite

Exercise is good. A little jogging, a bit of weight lifting, a spot of tennis, a round of golf. You burn a few calories, so you can reward yourself by eating more than usual. And if you burn a lot of calories, you are entitled to eat a LOT more than usual.

If anyone comments about how much you are overeating, you can reply with, *"It comes right off when I work out."*

Dessert
As a Metaphor for Life

A dessert is everything we want our lives to be—sweet, rewarding and fulfilling. We have successfully completed the hard work of eating a meal. Now, the prize—dessert. A true overeater raises dessert to a new height. An overeater is not tied to the tradition of having it only as the last dish of a dinner. Dessert first. Dessert for breakfast. Dessert any time of the day. Why not? And why not try every dessert offered? When it comes to dessert, just as in life, there is no reason to feel that something is missed. If you pass it up, it's gone forever.

CHAPTER 12
THE BIG PACIFIER

*"Home is where
the tart is."*

THE MISSING PEACE

While it is true that you can't put a square peg in a round hole, a cookie does fit quite nicely. Other circular shaped pieces of sugary goodness will also do the job of restoring peace and quiet when little mouths are open wide at crying time. Whether you use a lemon lollipop or a chocolate cupcake, it is a dollars to donuts certainty that a fussy child can't talk back or squeal when their mouth is full.

TABLE THAT DISCUSSION

Don't you wish that you could have a happy dinner table? Aren't you tired of conversations that begin and end with, *"Eat your vegetables." "Drink your milk." "Finish that fish." "Three more bites."* Why fight with pint-sized picky eaters? Just let them eat cake, cookies, ice cream and soda, and those pesky eating problems will disappear. Then, when table talk resumes, maybe you will be able to find out what they did in school that day.

More Free Time!

Tired of making snacks and meals for your children all the time? Looking for a way to build a few extra minutes of leisure into your jam-packed day? Putting a vending machine in your house—stocked with chips, cookies and hamburgers—will make chow time a no-brainer and teach your children added responsibility of taking care of themselves. And, when they spend their allowance on treats, you get your money back.

GETTING YOUR WAY
(BY GIVING THEM THEIRS)

Money isn't the only bribe that gets results. Food is just as effective. Everyone knows that from training their dog. Why not try it on your kid? Some simple strategies include, *"If you do your homework, we will go to your favorite fast-food restaurant." "Be nice to your sister, and you can have dessert for dinner." "If you take out the trash, I'll pack you a donut for lunch."* Who needs a high-priced behavioral counselor? Bribe that young one with food and you'll have the perfect child.

WHAT'S REALLY IMPORTANT

Pop Candy Chip Cookie

Overeaters have their priorities straight. It's a way to spend as much quality time as possible with the family. It's grocery shopping with your kids rather than going to the movies. It's watching the Food Network together, not the History Channel®. It's rewarding the kids with ice cream rather than money. Plus, think of how much extra together time you can share by serving course after course after course at a long and food-filled meal. Food always helps those family ties bind. Years from now, your children will remember those

FOOD FACTS

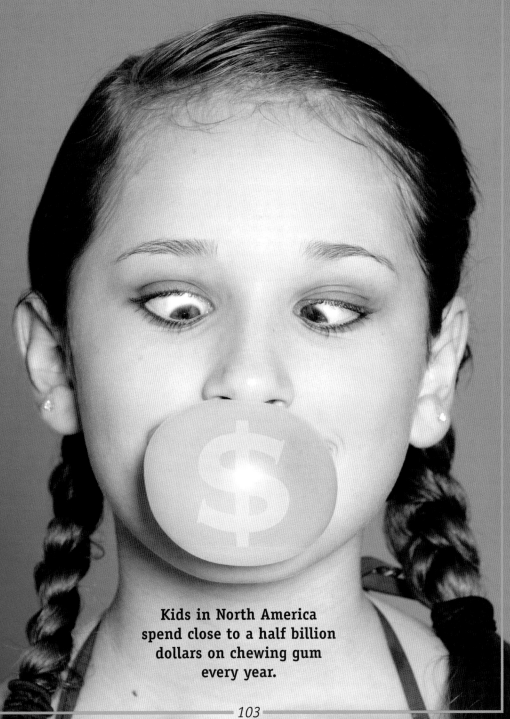

Kids in North America
spend close to a half billion
dollars on chewing gum
every year.

CHAPTER 13
BIGGER & BETTER

"*And they all ate
happily ever after.*"

Proof of the Pudding

(or Pizza or Pie or ...)

If overeating is bad, then why are there so many eating competitions across America? One group holds seventy contests a year. You can test your overeating prowess on matzoh balls in Houston, oysters in New Orleans (the "Big" Easy, naturally) or hot dogs in New York. What could be better? Stuff yourself with something you love and win money doing it ... it's the pot of mousse at the end of the rainbow.

FOOD FACTS

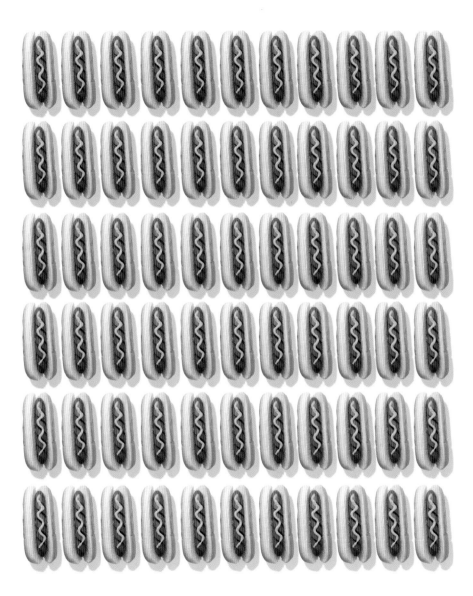

2007 World Record:
sixty-six **hot dogs (with buns)**
in twelve **minutes**

DIETS ARE GOOD

It is wonderful that there are so many different diets. Just remember that you don't have to choose just one. Try them all at the same time. That way, if one diet doesn't work, maybe another will. And you will never miss out on important vitamins and nutrients. You'll be getting your protein, your carbs, your unsaturated fat, your saturated fat, your sugar. There is something in every diet for everyone. Why not be a pioneer and take advantage of them all?

YOU'LL NEVER NEED TO EAT AGAIN!

FAT WILL FALL RIGHT OFF THE BONE!

LOSE-ITOL

ALL IS LOST!

500 CAPSULES OF ETERNAL THINNESS

"Foodie" Redefined

A "foodie" is today's "in" slang for a gourmet. Don't let anyone say you aren't a real foodie just because you'll eat anything in sight and in reach. That doesn't mean you don't appreciate fine food. Of course you do. Better yet, you are a connoisseur of all food, from potato latkes to pate. What could be more "foodie" than that?

THE FOOD CIRCLE

FROZEN POT PIE

GARLIC BREAD

THIN MINTS

DILL PICKLES

MAYONNAISE SANDWICH

SALAMI SLICES

SALT & VINEGAR CHIPS

FUDGE POP

Could there *be* anything more annoying than the food pyramid? Talk about government interference! The food police put all the delicious stuff on the itty bitty tip of the thing and then make you feel bad about eating too much of it. At the base, where the pyramid is big enough for a banana split, they put everything that no one wants to eat—lettuce, leaves, roots and such. Instead of the food pyramid, we need the more democratic food circle. Then all food will be equal and we can feel good about eating whatever we want in any amount we want. It will be a true merry-go-round of food.

FOOD FACTS

Peanuts are one
of the ingredients
in dynamite.

CHAPTER 14
THE BIG ADVANTAGE

*"The devil made
me chew it."*

It is time to stop thinking about overeating as a bad activity. In comparison to other popular passions, there are only benefits to overeating. So just think of it as "Column A" all the way!

Overeating vs. Sex

Culinary indulgence is better than the carnal kind because:

1. You can do it in public.
2. You can post photos of it on the Internet.
3. You can do it with your clothes on.
4. You can do it with everyone you know.
5. You can do it every five minutes.
6. Your hair doesn't get messed up.
7. You won't get an STD.
8. Food is never too tired.

Overeating vs. Drinking

Eating too much is far preferable to consuming too much alcohol because:

1. Driving While Eating (DWE) is legal.

2. It's OK to do it alone.

3. You will remember everything the next day.

4. Pepperoni breath will never get you busted.

5. There are no TV shows for "The Biggest Drinker."

6. Leftovers are better than hangovers.

7. Food fights are more fun than bar fights.

8. Rehab is very expensive.

Overeating vs. Shopping

Shopping for clothes is fun, but food shopping - and overeating - is more fun because:

1. You never have to try food on.

2. You will never have to return what you eat.

3. You won't have to look in the mirror while you eat.

4. Pizza never goes out of style.

5. Better to finger a rib rack than to fight a sale rack.

6. They can't put a security tag on a cinnamon roll.

7. The food court is centralized – no bothersome walking.

8. The food market is never out of your size.

Overeating vs. Cosmetic Surgery

While cosmetic surgery fulfills the body fantasy, overeating fills the tummy reality. Overeating is better than nipping and tucking because:

1. People won't have to pretend you look good.
2. Everyone will be able to see where your money went.
3. You can't have wrinkles with a full face.
4. You won't have to have a "redo" in five years.
5. You will have extra money for a new "larger" wardrobe.
6. Your face won't feel tight when you chew.
7. You won't have to hide out for weeks. In fact, you won't be able to hide at all.
8. Bigger breasts, the natural way.

FOOD FACTS

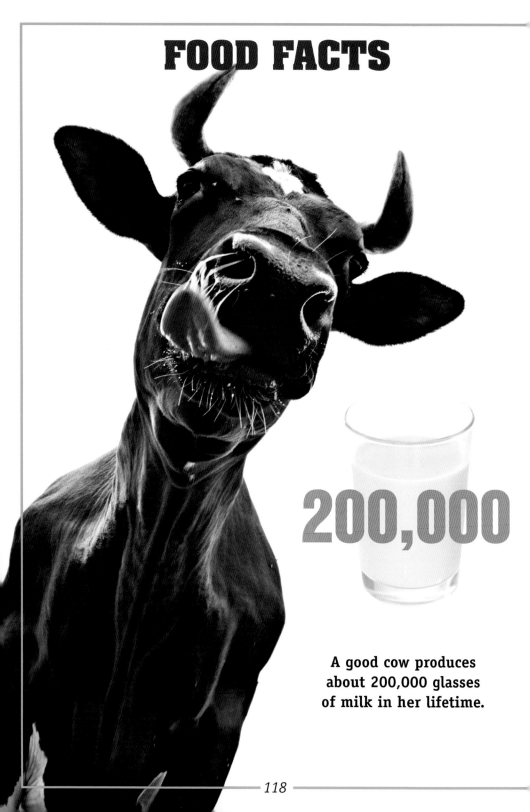

200,000

A good cow produces about 200,000 glasses of milk in her lifetime.

FOOD FACTS

A bee produces only
one twelfth of a teaspoon
of honey in its entire lifetime.

CHAPTER 15
THE BIG PAYOFF

"*Keep your eye upon the donut until you eat it whole.*"

Crazy Omar's
TENT EMPORIUM

A FISCAL CONSERVATIVE

Overeating can save you a lot of money. You will never have a second wardrobe of "thin" clothes a size too small.

The Value
(To The World)
Of Overeating

Overeating provides a vital function in this world. Food doesn't go to waste. There are far fewer leftovers to deal with and less garbage for the landfill. Refrigerators are cleaned out. Dishes are easier to wash. Restaurants do well. Supermarkets thrive. Farmers carry on. Doctors and hospitals have more patients. The diet industry gets rich. The economy is boosted. Overeaters are the real heroes of society.

The Golden Rule 2.0
Heaven can wait.

Dinner can not.

CHAPTER 16

THE BIG END

"*All's well that ends well fed.*"

MAÑANA I

If you didn't get to eat as much as you wanted today,
there's always tomorrow.

MAÑANA 2

In case there is no tomorrow,
        eat everything you can today.

APPENDICITIS

"" *The best things in life are fried.* ""

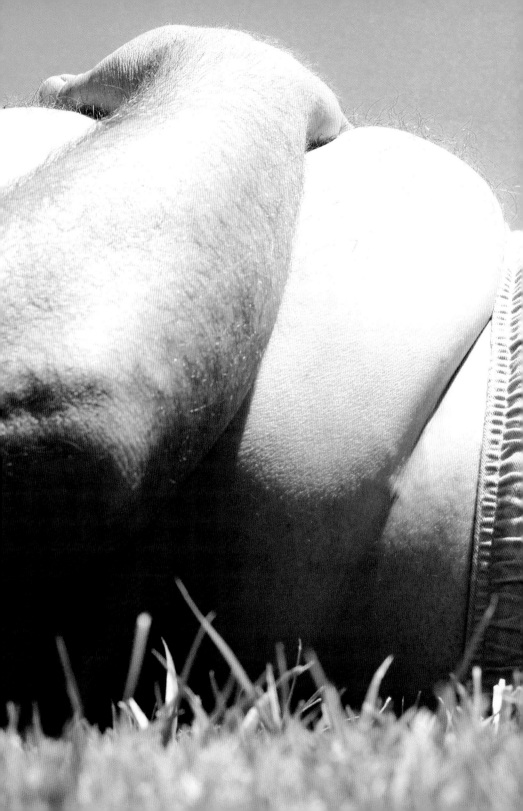

"America the Bountiful"

(sung to the tune of "America the Beautiful")

O plentiful are apple pies,
With sweetened scoops of cream,
And chocolate coated strawberries
That bust our clothing's seams!
America! America!
We gorge yes you and me,
And throw food wrappers on the streets
From sea to shining sea!

O bountiful are fatty steaks
That clog our arteries
They go so well with fried crab cakes
Until our heart valves seize!
America! America!
We make our waists expand
And show ourselves no self-control
With burgers in each hand!

O plentiful are cheesy chips
Piled high with bacon bits
A buffet blessed with endless dips
Across the bulging States!
America! America!
Do let us forge ahead
By leading others everywhere
In being overfed!

O bountiful our great expanse,
With fast food far and wide,
Huge courses splitting countless pants
Baked, battered and deep fried!
America! America!
Go make your buttered toast
And have your please with calories
From coast to groaning coast!

by Leslie Landis and Laura Grover

" It is not important whether you eat to live or live to eat. What is important is to laugh while you are eating. It aids in digestion. "

ABOUT THE AUTHOR

Leslie Landis has an M.A. in Clinical Psychology and is a licensed Marriage and Family Therapist. She lives on a sunny hillside in southern California with her husband and dog. Both have been major inspirations for her observations on overeating. She considers herself the ultimate "foodie" of kids' comfort food and makes the best peanut butter and jelly sandwich in the world.